Make All Communication TED-Worthy

Become a far more effective Leader and Communicator
By Using Principles Based in Neurobiology

Public speaking is the original human communication medium. Long before television and radio everything important started with public speaking. It's *still* the most effective method for influencing human beings and you're now in competition for people's attention with the best speakers in the world.

In this deeply insightful Itty Bitty Book, John Bates shows you how to use the powerful principles he teaches to TED and TEDx speakers, the NASA astronauts, top executives, and other leaders around the world.

You will:

- Discover the incredible power of mirror neurons as applied to public speaking and leadership.
- Experience the amazing difference when you use advice from none other than Snoop Doggy Dogg.
- Learn the 3 ways to inspire and connect with any audience, any time, any place on Earth.

If becoming a TED speaker interests you pick up this important itty bitty book today.

Your Amazing Itty Bitty® Guide to Being TED-Worthy

15 Essential Secrets of Successful Speaking Based in Human Neurobiology

John-Alfred Kohler Bates

Published by Itty Bitty® Publishing
A subsidiary of S & P Productions, Inc.

Copyright © 2018 **John A. K. Bates**

All rights reserved. No part of this book may be reproduced or transmitted in any form or by any means, electronic or mechanical, including photocopying, recording or by any information storage and retrieval system, without written permission of the publisher, except for inclusion of brief quotations in a review.

Printed in the United States of America

Itty Bitty Publishing
311 Main Street, Suite D
El Segundo, CA 90245
(310) 640-8885

TED did not produce or promote this book.

Cover Photo: ©Marla Aufmuth/TED
marlaaufmuth.com (JKB)

ISBN: 978-1-950326-21-1

I dedicate this book to all of the amazing people I met both in the TED organization and at TED conferences over the years. I'm particularly grateful to Kelly Young Stoetzel – you transformed my life by creating TEDActive. And, to Chris Anderson whose generosity of spirit and utterly courageous approach to freeing the information and Ideas Worth Spreading of TED to the whole wide world has radically changed the whole wide world. Also, thank you Benjamin Zander! Our accidental collaboration while singing Happy 25th Birthday to TED in 2009 put me onto a path I couldn't have even dreamed of back then. And, to Simon Sinek whose TEDx talk is one of the most popular TED talks ever, for generously taking his time to help me finally nail my WHY at TEDActive in 2014 – Wow, what a difference that made. And, finally, I dedicate this to YOU for having the courage to step through the natural fear we all have of being noticed, to do what it will take to clarify and hone your message, and then... to go out and share YOUR idea worth spreading. I can't wait for the world to hear it. Best of Luck!

- John Bates

Stop by our Itty Bitty® website Directory to find interesting TEDx information from our experts.

www.IttyBittyPublishing.com

Or visit our Expert at:

ExecutiveSpeakingSuccess.com

**Table of Essential Secrets
To Being TED-Worthy**

Secret 15. Say Yes To Your Opportunity To Make A Difference

Introduction by Mike Michalowicz

The best way to compliment an awesome itty-bitty guide that will get you speaking on the TED platform, is to have an itty-bitty foreword. So, that is my intention here – short and to the point.

What you are about to experience in John Bates' book are the exact methods I have used. As a result, I have had the privilege to speak on the TED platform multiple times, to deliver mainstage keynotes at the largest entrepreneurial conferences in the world, and to have a flourishing career as a speaker.

I have experienced all that, and more, because of the exact lessons that are contained within this book that is now in your hands. These techniques took me years to discover. First on my own, and then ultimately from John, when I hired him as my speaking coach.

For over ten years he has been my guide, showing me how to improve my presentations each time. My only wish is that he published this book sooner, because I would have reviewed and revisited it time and time again before every speech. And, now that this book has been released, that is my plan.

In these pages John will show you why as a speaker, you are not a speaker – you are a performer.

You are privileged with the ultimate platform of influence, and you are expected to bring the best of you to every single performance. You are in the position to change lives.

Commit to mastering the principles contained in this book. Commit to bringing the best of you every time you speak. Commit to reviewing this guide every time before you step on stage. The audience is starving for your greatness. This book will show you how to bring it.

> Mike Michalowicz – Best Selling Author of *Profit First*, TV Personality, International Speaker & Entrepreneur

Essential Secret # 1
What is Your ONE Idea Worth Spreading?

TED is deservedly popular for a lot of reasons. One of the big ones is that the talks are short and focused. Even non-TED speakers can benefit from that lesson! Every time I have been coached by TED the number one thing that stands out for me is their repetition of the question: What is your one idea worth spreading?

1. It's not your two or three best ideas. The thing you must answer for yourself if you want to be successful is: What is the one, singular idea to which you are going to dedicate *this* talk. After that, everything else you say must line up behind that one, main point like the shaft of a Neolithic spear behind its flinty point.

2. One way to get in touch with your idea is to ask yourself the question: If I knew, in my heart of hearts, that the world would really listen to me for 5, 10, 18 minutes, what is the one idea I would most want to share?

3. Do not get all hung up on finding the one, right idea. You probably have more than one and the right one is the one you pick.

Explore Your Ideas and Then Pick One.

Find your idea. Feel free to explore the universe of possibilities but set a time limit for this exploration, a day, or a week, so your talk doesn't die of "perfection paralysis."

- Drop the thought that you have one perfect idea. You have many. Explore them and then pick one! It's the one!
- In Hollywood they call the first draft of a screenplay throwing up on the page. Creating an awful first draft is WAY better than the non-existent perfect first draft. Start throwing up!
- Imagine what would actually matter to the audience. Think about what you'd say to someone you love and respect most in the world if they asked you for one of your most powerful insights.
- Some people are very clear about what their "TED talk" would be. Others are much less clear. I believe you've got a TED-worthy talk inside you if you're willing to be authentic and really dig deep
- Often the people with whom I work created great talks. But, I can tell there's another level; something deeper, and I make them go digging, again. If you feel like there's something even deeper, dig again, it makes for some of the best talks.

Essential Secret # 2
Make Time To Do This Right, Or Don't Do It Until You Can Make Time To Do It Right

Most of my life, when I had 3 months to prepare I would pretend to ponder, work on and think about my talk while I actually was resisting and procrastinating. It is an awful experience. To actually live up to your true potential takes time.

1. Talks consume human life. 1 person speaking for 20 minutes to 3000 people uses up 60,000 minutes – divide by 60 and that is 1,000 hours of human life. If you want your talk to be well received and even go viral, dedicate some of your own time, up front.
2. If you have 3 months, get your talk finalized within the first two weeks. Then you have 2.5 months to live with, practice, polish and refine your talk.
3. When you put that kind of effort into your talk you end up being an "expert" in your talk. That expertise rubs off on everything else about you. That's a good thing and it will probably amaze you.
4. Almost no one else is doing this. When you do you look totally amazing.

You Walk Off the Stage Feeling One of Two Ways. Awesome or Awful.

Every time you take the stage you get to choose how it is going to go. Awesome is, well, awesome! And awful is one of the lowest, worst feelings in the world. I've done both, awesome is definitely better, and it's worth the work.

- After crafting his speeches, Steve Jobs used a formula. He would practice an *hour* for every *minute* of his speech. A 45 minute speech would get 45 hours of practice time. No wonder people call him a "natural communicator."
- Practicing out loud is extremely important. As you hear yourself you'll be much better at refining and tweaking.
- Practice your speech in front of people you respect and love. Practice your speech in front of the dog, the cat, the mirror, the wall, the window. Practice!
- There is an art to getting feedback on your speech. Always, always, always say, "Thank you!" And then, be judicious about what suggestions you actually incorporate. Everyone wants to be helpful, but it's your speech and not all suggestions are equally good for your speech.
- It's a lot easier to get to the "deeper level" talk if you start early, in earnest.

Essential Secret # 3
How to Create a Great Speech Without Suffering

Once you've got an idea about your idea it's time for a brain dump. Finish this itty bitty book before you start this, but it's good to be able to envision the process, now Write out your ideas by putting one, and only one idea, story, or point you want to make, on one Post-It Note. Do this near a big, blank wall and stick them up as fast as you write them. Once you have all your ideas, points and stories out, go through and pull the best ones to another part of the wall; the Curation Phase.

1. Prioritizing is one of the most intensive and difficult activities that your brain can perform, but this phase is one big key to a truly great talk or presentation.
2. Keep the leftovers! They're the starter culture for your next talk.
3. Go through what you have curated and look for the best order in which to share them.
4. Make the flow logical, but not predictable. Use the storytelling techniques you learn later on the talk structure, as well.
5. Now, either create an outline, or, write it out word for word. This is very personal and up to you. I do it both ways, depending.

Keep Someone You Deeply Love and Respect in Mind As You Do This

Now, practice going through your speech, *out loud*. Notice, I haven't said time it, yet! Don't worry about time, yet. Once you have the main idea of the speech rolling you can start to think more about time. Obviously, if it's got to be 12 minutes and you're at 45, you might want to go back to the Post-It Notes. But, better to trim it down later than to miss the gold by leaving something key out too early.

- CAUTION: If you write it out word for word be sure it is written like you speak, not like you write! Well "written" speeches draw the worst kind of ire from audiences. Once you have it where you want it it's best to turn it into an outline and practice from that, unless you have lots of time to perfect it word for word can easily come off insincere.
- Now, if you want to be really extraordinary, you will go back and dig even deeper. Ask yourself, what am I avoiding telling people? What am I afraid of sharing? What if I let my guard down?
- Now that you've got the real thing, and not before, start thinking about whether or not you even need any slides.

Essential Secret # 4
Include Your Superhero Origin Story & Establish "Emotional Credibility"™

One of the most extraordinary things you can do for the audience is to share yourself, the right way. Don't focus on Superhero, focus instead on *origin* story. We want to know what connects you to your subject, why you care, so we can care, too.

1. You are where you are, doing what you're doing because you made all the choices that led you here. Every time you could have done this or that, you did this and it led you here. We want to know something about one of the places you made a difficult choice and why you chose this over that.

2. Forget establishing your credibility. You're on stage speaking! Your credibility is already established. What's important, you'll clearly see why later in this book, is to establish your "Emotional Credibility"™.

3. People will connect with you when you share the things that went through your mind as you navigated that difficult choice. People want to know!

Step Out With Confidence in Yourself

Studies show that when you have letters after your name like PhD, MD, CPA, your credibility is assumed. I think it's fair to say that extends to situations where you were picked to be on stage, or you are the CEO, VP and so on. People are not moved to action by logic, as you'll see later. The emotional connection is what does that.

- If your credibility is already assumed, trying to establish your credibility on top of that actually tarnishes your credibility.
- Sharing your decision making process gives people an insight into how your mind and heart work. That is important information and allows us to feel like we know you better.

Sharing some of your inner life is important if you want to be influential and truly connect.

- What were the things that you were weighing in the moment before you chose this over that?
- What are the things you value about the things you were weighing and why did this one win out over that one?
- Sharing your mental turmoil doesn't make you look bad. It actually makes you look self-aware.

Essential Secret # 5
Be Responsible for What They Hear

What do you mean? That's crazy. How can I be responsible for what another human being hears? All it takes, actually, is the realization that you'll be far more effective if you even try to take this on. It will dramatically alter how you approach the whole talk and it will definitely make it far better.

1. Take the time to get to know your audience, think about their world, their views, their experiences and how you could most effective say things so that they would hear them.
2. If you can talk to some of the people who will be in your audience take the opportunity to do so. Ask them questions, run some of your ideas past them and ask them how they land for them, and when they talk, listen like your life depends on it. The success of your talk certainly does.
3. Is there a different way you could open? Is the example you're using the most relevant one for them?

"Your presentation is not a presentation, it's a performance." – Michael Weiss

Being Responsible for What They Hear Will Probably Change How You Say It.

Once, when I was speaking to a group of extremely high performing young girls in Estonia I purposefully began my talk by telling them I didn't think I had much to say to them that they'd value. "After all," I said, "I'm a man, I'm an American, I'm much older than you are..." At first, they looked at me with great consternation, but then they started making the argument that I did have something relevant to share with them and that they wanted me to do so. Of course, I wasn't too hard to convince, but I'm sure that opening like that had them listening in a much more powerful way than they might have, otherwise.

- What do you know about your audience and how can you use that to more powerfully land your message?
- How can you get to know your audience better? Can you manage to set up an interview with some of the stakeholders before you craft your talk? Can you spend some time with audience members any time before you give you talk? Even simply mingling with them the night before can make a big difference in how you can approach things.

Essential Secret # 6
Don't Tell The Whole Story! Curate Your Knowledge!

Imagine a rummage store that is filled to the brim with stuff. Every nook and cranny and flat surface is just packed with stuff. Now, imagine that stuff is everything you know.

Guess what, I don't want to know all that! And, you don't want me to know all that, either. If I knew all that I'd be you and maybe even competing for your job. I don't want to know all of that stuff... I just want the treats!

1. "I sometimes get into the weeds," is one of the hallmarks of an ineffective speaker and leader. But, there's hope!
2. It's really easy to make something complicated even more complicated. The art of great communication is making something complicated simple and elegant.

You see, you're the expert. That's why you get paid the big bucks. You know all of that stuff *and* you know your audience. Now, it's incumbent upon you to curate your knowledge and only share with the audience the things they need and want to know, what I call the treats!

Your Poetic License

To those who read these words, greetings. Be it known that the bearer of this parchment has complete poetic license, in service of the audience.

They are hereby allowed to NOT tell the whole story, to treat the rules of grammar as malleable, and to forego their ego in service of the AUDIENCE.

- Don't include anything that is not actually important to the audience.
- Your ability to get into the weeds is fine in QA, but it actually dramatically decreases your effectiveness when you're presenting.

The other night my wife and I had this absolutely amazing dinner… I think it was Friday night… No, was it Saturday night? Gee, maybe it could have been Thursday night…
"I *don't care* what night it was! Tell me about the dinner!"

- Yes, even the rules of grammar are malleable in service of the audience!
- Only include the things that really matter.

Visit ExecutiveSpeakingSuccess.com/poetic for your very own printable copy of your poetic license.

Essential Secret # 7
The Essential Power of Story

Throughout our history as a species, up until the printing press, how did everything important, and I mean everything, get shared and passed on? Orally. Verbally. Right. But, it wasn't just long lists of stuff. Studies show we can't remember more than 4 bits of information and that's not enough to build great buildings, or succeed at agriculture, or brew beer. No, it was oral, but it had to be in the form of a story! The power of story is how humanity managed to grow and preserve our store of knowledge. So, it makes sense that our brains would come to more highly value story than anything else in communication! Two of the cardinal rules of effective communication are:

1. Never tell a story without a point.
2. And, never make a point without a story!

That can seem like a high bar, but it's absolutely worth aiming for if what you're saying matters and if you want people to remember what you say and take action on it.

What is the story you can tell that will illustrate the point you want to convey? You have more personal stories than you likely realize.

Our Brains Value Story More Highly Than Anything Else in Communication

That's worth repeating and remembering. We are hard wired to respond to stories. Think of a great leader you have worked with. Did they ever tell you a story you remember? Does it still impact you to this day? I'll wager money the answer is yes because you're a human being and that's how we work.

- When people listen to stories their brains light up in in an fMRI in the same way as when they expect to receive a reward.
- Well told stories with a point are like nuggets of gold you can give to anyone you meet. Your stories are valuable.

Many of us were taught in school not to fall for anecdotal evidence. In other words, don't think one story proves something. That's good advice, but the flip side of that advice is that if you have good data, or an honestly useful point to make, and you don't enlist the assistance of a story then you're missing out on the #1 tool for communicating with human beings that exists anywhere. Period.

- Create a story-catcher, wherein you can jot notes about your stories. Then, when you need a new story to illustrate some point, you can reference your story-catcher and pick something good.

Essential Secret # 8
Creating Great Stories, Two Techniques

OK, stories are strikingly important, but most people I talk with think they're not very good storytellers! They're wrong! Story is so important to us as human beings that it has shaped our evolution. If you didn't have what it takes to be a good storyteller genetically built into you already you'd have been plucked from the gene pool already, generations ago. You have what it takes, but you might not know it, yet. Here are two very powerful techniques to bring out your spellbinding inner storyteller.

1. In Medias Res. This is an ancient Greek technique that all the latest movies are using. It means: into the middle things and the basic idea is start in the middle.
2. Present tense. It's not for every story and it's diabolically difficult to do at first, but the right stories told in present tense will absolutely work magic for you.

These two techniques, when practiced and combined will elevate your ability to absolutely captivate any audience. In medias res perks up their curiosity and present tense literally pulls them into the moment right alongside you.

Don't Give It Away Too Soon

When you're looking for a place to start in the middle a great place to begin is somewhere that will pique people's curiosity and make them want to find out what's going to happen. So, you can't give it away too soon! Set it up, draw us in and then go back to how it all got to this point, and only relieve the curiosity tension when it serves to help you make your point.

- Imagine, it's 3 years ago, I'm on the African Savannah and monkeys are falling out of the sky, vs, I wanted to go to Africa to see the tree that has fruit that ferments on the branches because I heard the animals all come and get drunk...
- Remember, our curiosity will have us hang in there through all kinds of things to find out what will happen. Don't spill the beans too early.

Present tense is as difficult as it is powerful. You wouldn't just walk out on stage and juggle running chainsaws in front of an audience for the first time. Present tense requires practice.

- Once you have your present tense story record yourself telling it and notice if you go back to past tense.
- Stay in present tense for the entire story and for every part of the story.

Essential Secret # 9
Core Neurobiology, Two Secrets

There are two fundamental pieces of neurobiology that are some of the most overlooked keys to success with human communication that exist. One is the paleomammalian brain and the other is mirror neurons. Master them and you will succeed beyond your wildest imagination.

1. The human brain has two basic and distinct structures; the paleomammalian brain and the neocortex. Action comes from the paleomammalian brain.
2. We all have mirror neurons which make us internally mirror the emotions we see in others. Are you driving that process, or falling victim to it?

The paleomammalian brain is the ancient brain. It has been around for a lot longer than the neocortex. It has its hands on the steering wheel of action and it does not have access to language or logic. It is deeply dialed into reality, however, and it notices things we'll never consciously notice; patterns, smells, pheromones, facial micro gestures, and more. It can't talk to us, so it communicates thorough "gut feelings.'

Put Neurobiology to Work for You

Most people think they make logical choices. Wrong. If we put you in an fMRI machine and watched your brain as you made a decision we'd see the paleomammalian brain fire first, making the decision, and the logical neocortex would fire immediately afterwards, agreeing or disagreeing, but not making the decision. We must reach the paleomammalian brain to elicit a yes, or cause action.

- You must make an emotional connection or your logic will simply bounce off.
- Give them something good to mirror and they will!
- Being nervous and focused on yourself is not something you want them to mirror.

Yes we like it, yes it's priced right, yes it would make a difference, no we're not ready to buy... Have you had a similar experience? Yes, yes, yes no? What happened? Logic, logic, logic, emotion. We didn't connect with and put the paleomammalian brain at ease. So, the logical part of the brain got shut out.

- Establish your Emotional Credibility™ to create an opening for your audience to take action, feel loyalty, respect, and more.
- Be as relaxed and present as you want them to be. They will mirror you.

Essential Secret # 10
Public Speaking is Dangerous! This Helps.

I would be remiss if I didn't point out that public speaking is dangerous! That's why it's so nerve wracking. I mean, look at what happened to Jesus, and Joan of Arc, and Martin Luther King and John F. Kennedy, and on and on! They got noticed by the group and then look what happened. There's a name for people who are not at all afraid of public speaking; sociopath. It makes sense to be afraid of public speaking, actually. The point is not to be fearless, that would get you killed even faster, the point is to be courageous; have your fear and be willing to step through it for something that matters to you.

1. If you have a public speaking event that doesn't matter to you, don't do it! Public speaking is dangerous.
2. If you have a public speaking event that does matter to you, don't beat yourself up for being nervous.

Please remember that when you say no to an opportunity to speak in public you're also saying no to your opportunity to make a difference, period. So what if you don't think you're enough of an expert. They think you are! Go with it.

Courage is Stepping Through Your Fear

I got some of the best advice ever, for public speaking and for life, from two very different sources. One is Snoop Dogg, no kidding. The other is a globally recognized leadership trainer named Candace. They said it differently, but it's the same advice.

- Snoop said, "Don't be nervous, be at their service..." That's brilliant and poetic.
- Candace said, "If you get up on stage and you're attention is on yourself, then your attention is on a minor ball of petty concerns that is of no interest to anyone but you." Ouch. "But, if you get up on stage and your attention is on your message and the audience, and the difference you're going to make for them and the difference they'll make out in the world, because of it, well now your attention is on something worth thinking about!"

Nervous is all about you. Stop being so narcissistic <wink>. Focus on your message and the "nervous" becomes "excited."

- Bullet point more stuff about step 9

Essential Secret # 11
How to Connect with and Inspire Any Audience, Anywhere, Any Time.

Being able to do that is tremendously powerful and useful in any setting that includes human beings. If you include each of these in your talk it will be an out of the ballpark hit every time.

1. People don't connect with your successes. They connect with your messes. Your message is in your mess. - Les Brown
2. Don't make yourself special. Make the process special. – Craig Valentine
3. Don't be the hero of your own talk. Make the audience the hero. – Nancy Duarte

They work very well in that order, too. The first one demonstrates humility and self-awareness. It also takes great courage to be that authentic. The second one is a great way to be able to share some successes without alienating the audience. People can't relate to you if you're special, but they love processes that produce success. And, the third is a great way to send them out! If they answer your call to action they can be heroes in their own lives.

Truly Inspiring

There are two kinds of inspiring. One is the kind that goes like this: You're so amazing… I could never be like you. Not actually inspiring, but it masquerades as inspiring too often. The second goes like this: You're so amazing… Maybe if I did what you did I could be great like you. That is truly inspiring.

When you do that people get something valuable, vs. just being left with you and your specialness, which doesn't help them at all.

- It's not about whining, it's about sharing a real, painful, embarrassing event and *what you learned* from it. That is absolute gold to an audience. Don't cover up the hurt. It's important to the experience and cements the lesson.
- I won tons of contests doesn't help the audience. I won tons of contests because I had a great coach and I was coachable does! Share the process.
- When they do what you are asking them to do they can be heroes in their own lives. That's a win for everyone.

Incorporating these three things into every speech you deliver will give the audience a real gift and make you stand out in the best of ways.

Essential Secret # 12
The TED Commandments Make ANY Speech Better.

1. Thou Shalt Not Trot Out Thy Usual Schtick
2. Thou Shalt Dream A Great Dream Or Show Forth A Wondrous New Thing, Or Share Something Thou Hast Never Shared Before.
3. Thou Shalt Reveal Thy Curiosity And Thy Passion.
4. Thou Shalt Tell A Story
5. Thou Shalt Freely Comment On The Utterances Of Other Speakers For The Sake Of Blessed Connection And Exquisite Controversy
6. Thou Shalt Not Flaunt They Ego, Be Thou Vulnerable. Speak Of They Failures As Well As Thy Success
7. Thou Shalt Not Sell From The Stage Neither Thy Company Nor They Desperate Need For Funding Lest Though Be Cast Aside Into Outer Darkness
8. Thou Shalt Remember All The While Laughter Is Good
9. Thou Shalt Not Read Thy Speech
10. Thou Shalt Not Steal The Time Of Them That Follow Thee.

Apply the TED Commandments

If you follow these commandments it will make all of your presentations far better. If you're doing a TED format talk it is *essential* that you follow these commandments.

- If you're speaking at a TED event and you trot our your usual schtick it will fail, even if your usual schtick is really good.
- Instead, what is like to be the person who does what you do all the time? What has doing this taught you that you haven't shared yet? Go up to 50K feet, come down to 500 feet. Give us something different.

Notice the many, extremely important pieces in the TED Commandments that most talks lack.

- Dreaming, curiosity and passion revealed Hint: if you're passionate you have to tell your face!
- Storytelling, connection, vulnerability
- No selling, ego or reading your talk

This is one of the reasons TED has taken over our consciousness so much. It's just good stuff. And, one of the really big deals at TED is staying within your allotted time. It's gluttony to consume the time allotted to others. Don't do it.

Essential Secret # 13
The Bates Equation Of Public Speaking

1 x 20 x 3000 = 60,000. That's me, speaking for 20 minutes to 3000 people. 60,000 minutes. Divide by 60 and we get 1000 hours of human life that I am consuming with one, twenty minute talk to 3000 people. And, I don't want to practice? Well, I didn't, until I went to TED and found out that many of the most popular speakers had practiced for a year or more.

1. If you have 12 weeks before a speech give yourself a hard deadline of two weeks to create the speech. Then, spend the remaining 10 practicing, polishing and perfecting it.
2. When you deliver your speech like an expert (because you've spent so much time practicing it) people automatically, unconsciously think you're an expert, in general. That is a huge reward for becoming an expert in your speech.
3. Put this in your daytime calendar. If you do it Sunday morning before the kids wake up you'll never actually do it, and if you do it'll never be as good as it could be. This is worth making time for. You *will* regret not enough time spent. You will never regret too much time spent.

How To Be A "Natural Communicator"

I work with a very good friend who worked closely with Steve Jobs for many years. Did you know that after working very hard with his team to craft a great speech, Steve Jobs would then practice an hour for every minute that he was going to be on stage? No wonder people call him a natural communicator!

- Record yourself audio in the early stages, video, later. Your smart phone works just fine for this!
- Watch and listen to yourself like you're listening to a very close, dear friend. If you listen like it's you there's a good chance you'll be so hard on yourself it will be a counterproductive experience.
- Debrief these recordings like the Blue Angels do: Spend 20% of your time looking at and fixing the things that don't work and 80% of your time celebrating what does work. Yes, I'm serious.

There is a place where you can practice so much it seems like you practiced a lot. Not the goal. To get over that valley of awkwardness it just takes more practice.

- Even if you're good, you will never reach peak potential winging it. Practice so much it seems like you didn't practice at all.

Essential Secret # 14
On Stage Do This, Don't Do That

There are three main mistakes I see my clients make over and over, before we work together. The biggest is non-purposeful movement.

1. I have never seen anyone who walked, wandered or fidgeted too little during a 20-minute speech. Almost everyone wanders, stalks or sways and massively detracts from the impact they could have.

2. If you plant your feet, bend your knees a little so you don't faint, and then make sure you turn your face in the direction of all audience members during your speech, that would be find.

3. If you walk, make it mean something; walk because you're transitioning, or saying something that relates to and calls for movement.

4. Yes, use your hands as you talk. People *need* to see your hands the entire time. I can't emphasize this strongly enough. When your hands disappear behind your back, or into a pocket, people subconsciously check out. They're worried about what you're doing with your hands. It will kill your message.

Credibility Is Created

Credibility is the outcome of many factors. Besides actually being credible, factors you can control that have a huge impact are eye contact and not speaking too quickly.

- The audience is made up of individuals. Talk to them like you're in a serial one on one conversation with them.
- A huge part of that is eye contact. Our eyes are very conspicuous for a reason. People can tell whether you're looking at them or not. Make eye contact, deliver a thought, slide your gaze to the next 1:1 conversation and deliver your next line or two, swing your gaze to the next 1:1 conversation, and so on. Make eye contact with someone in all parts of the room as you do this.

The studies on delivery make it very clear that the best pace for a speech is either conversational or a very, tiny bit faster than conversational. Keep it conversational. Use powerful pauses. Practice.

- Fast speakers are rated as not knowing their subject, not being trustworthy and as low status.
- Slower speakers are rated as being experts, being trustworthy and high status.

Essential Secret # 15
Say Yes To Your Opportunity to Make a Difference.

I trained the speakers and spoke at TEDxTaiz, in Yemen. They had 50/50 men and women on stage in a country not known for their support of women's rights. When I asked my friends who organize TEDx events in the US and Europe how come we usually have something more like 60/40 they all said the same thing. When we ask 10 men to speak, 9 say yes. When we ask 10 women to speak, 9 say no. There are possibly good reasons for this, sometimes. But, in my experience and research, it's usually something like, "I'm not enough of an expert yet," that takes both women, and some men, out.

1. When you say no to your opportunity to speak, you are also, unequivocally saying no to your opportunity to make a difference. Period.
2. If they think you're enough of an expert, or that you have something worthwhile to say, isn't it a bit narcissistic of you to tell them you know better than they do? <wink> Just give it your best and make a difference.
3. Refer back to Essential Secret #10

Stay Focused on the Audience, the Message and Making a Difference

It's easy to get caught up in what a difference speaking, at TEDx or elsewhere, can make for you. Of course. It certainly can. And, as counterintuitive as it may sound, the way to make the biggest difference for yourself it to focus on making the biggest difference for your audience.

- What you want to share is important, yes. And, is it really what will make the biggest difference for the audience?
- People naturally want to reciprocate. If you try to sell them, they'll try to sell you. If you freely give them a huge gift they want to do the same for you.

As a final point, the beginning and the ending are arguably the most important parts of your speech. Do not open with things like thank you for having me, it's a real honor, etc.

- Ask yourself, "what is the exciting, engaging, make them want to listen way I'm going to open?"
- Set up a cliffhanger, ask a highly engaging question, make a bold promise. Grab their attention.

And, your closing should include your call to action, if you have one, and send them out thinking about the main point you want them to remember. All the best to you! Go get 'em, Tiger!

You've finished. Before you go…

Tweet/share that you finished this book.

Please star rate this book.

Reviews are solid gold to writers. Please take a few minutes to give us some itty bitty feedback.

ABOUT THE AUTHOR

John Bates has always had the soft skills and was, for a long time, envious of those with the hard skills. That is, until he first attended the TED Conference in 2009 where he was absolutely astounded by the power of truly great public speaking.

As he was volunteering for one of the very first TEDx events, TEDxSantaMonica, he had a light bulb moment. One of the speakers, who had all the hard skills, was so uncomfortable and nervous that everyone in the audience felt like they were going to throw up, because the speaker was so nervous. As the evil part of John laughed with schadenfreude, his good friend Michael Weiss walked over and said, "We've got to do something to make a difference for people like this…"

It was a liminal moment for John as he realized that if he just got over himself, he could make a difference for people, especially people with the hard skills.

Out of that experience John based all of his coaching and training in neurobiology and science so he could show people not only what works when it comes to communicating with human beings, but WHY it works, based in science. John is now one of the most prolific TED-Format trainers in the world. He works regularly with organizations like NASA, Boston

Scientific, Johnson & Johnson's JLABS and he has so far coached the speakers for over 35 TEDx events, and counting.

If you enjoyed this Amazing Itty Bitty® book you might also like…

- **Your Amazing Itty Bitty® How To Become A Keynote Speaker** – Lisa Haisha, M.A.

- **Your Amazing Itty Bitty® Fear-Busting Book** – Lucetta Zaytoun

- **Your Amazing Itty Bitty® Self-Esteem Book** – Jade Elizabeth

    Or any of the many other Itty Bitty® books available on line.

Made in the USA
Columbia, SC
04 July 2020

13252232R00026